SHATTERED

BEFORE THEY

BLOSSOMED

EB TAYLOR

SHATTERED BEFORE THEY BLOSSOMED

Copyright © 2022 EB Taylor

Printed by Amazon Inc., in the United States of America.

First printing, 2022

Lyla D Creations LLC
24445 Painter Drive
Land O Lakes, FL 34639

www.lyladcreations.com

Cover by Carter Cover Designs
Formatted by Carxander Publishing

Table of Contents

<u>PERFECT</u>

You were perfect to me.
Your smile,
Your eyes,
Your heart.
All perfect,
Until you weren't.

<u>LIE</u>

If you knowingly lie to a court,
You will lie to,
Your spouse,
Children,
Parents,
Friends,
Colleagues,
Strangers,
And yourself.
You will lie to
Anyone.

<u>SCARED</u>

I'm scared of what may happen.
I'm not what he thinks.
I'm scared of doing this alone.
I've never been here.
I'm scared of being labeled.
Something I'm not.
I'm scared.

It's time.
Not what she'd hoped for,
But it's time.
She only wanted to be seen and heard.
But this time,
That's not possible.
This time,
Their hearts weren't open.
This time,
She was fooled.

And,
Next time,
Oh, hell no.
There will never be a next time.

PROMISES

She made him promises.
No matter how much hurt he brings upon her,
No matter how many lies he says about her,
No matter how long he stays silent,
She will not break them.
It's her integrity.
She won't compromise it.
She'll live her life knowing she told the truth,
Causing pain to the one she truly loved,
But saving her soul.

<u>INTUITION</u>

I followed my intuition,
I wasn't the least bit scared.
I trusted my intuition.

What went wrong?
Was my intuition wrong about you?
Or was it right?
And you got scared.

Only you know those answers.
One day,
Will you share?

<u>CLOSURE</u>

I'm lost.
I need closure.
I can't function fully without it.
You'll burden me forever
Without closure.

<u>FELL</u>

She fell for him.
Hard, deep, real.
His eyes smiled at her.
His touch excited her.
His voice melted her.

When his arms embraced her,
She fell even further,
Into him.

It's not about wanting the other.
She wants,
He wants,
But they can't.

A love never hers was lost none the less.
The pain, tears, and heartbreak were all real.
He turned a cold black silence.

Putting her heart back together will take time.
Trying to let go and move on has begun
From a love never hers.

Something so beautiful
Became pure chaos.
It's all so unbelievable that she fell for him.
When he was a love never hers.

IMAGINATION

It's all in her imagination, they said.
She's made it all up.
Move on, let go.
Please stop telling her to do that.

She lived it.
She saw how he reacted to her.
He loved it.
He took it all in.
Enjoyed all the attention.
She's not exaggerating.
It was real.

He knows it but will deny it all.
He lies, not her.
He knows the truth will cause him trouble.
She'll be here when the lies finally catch up to him.
She'll be there for him.
She'll forgive him.
Because she knows the truth.

His sweetness melted her.
His touch aroused her.
His arms around her,
Set her on fire.

He wove a web around her heart.
Played along with her flirtatious way.
She fell deep.
Too deep to escape.

He turned on her,
His sweet web became ice.
He kicked her in the gut,
Dropped her off a cliff,
Became a viper before her very eyes,
As he poisoned her forever.

BOTTLE

She wants to crawl into a bottle,
And drown in its smooth liquid.
Let the bottle's caramel water
Take her away.
Wash away the fucking mess
That encompasses her life.
She begs, "please bottle,
Make me feel nothing,
Make me numb."

<u>NOT ME</u>

Brown hair,
Brown eyes.
That's not me.

The person calling your office,
Not me either.
That person following you,
Nope, not me.
The person you claim to fear,
Definitely not me.

But that person you lied about,
Yes,
That's me.

ALWAYS KNEW

She always knew they'd never be.
Many reasons prevented them.
She desired and hoped,
But always knew,
They'd never be.

Everyone deserves
A second chance.
I'm waiting
For mine.

LIFE

Life is joyous, spontaneous, fun.
Life is love, romantic, beautiful.
Everyone wants a nice long life.
Filled with family, friends, and love.

In a moment all that can change.
Life can be cruel, hard, contentious.
Life is unfair, unkind, ugly.
For some life is too short.

Fate can make life interesting,
Then karma can bite hard.

Life.
One day it is glorious, perfect.
The next day it's a mess, a wreck.

Life goes on
No matter what.

DOESN'T KNOW WHY

She doesn't know why she put such hope in him.
Maybe because he was so unbelievably caring at one
time.
Because he seemed to be an honest man.
He touched her in a way no one ever had.
It took her by surprise,
But she welcomed it.

She wanted more from him,
How much more?
She didn't know.
A friendship maybe.
She knew she wanted him to be a part of her life in some
way.

Now she must protect herself from him.
She doesn't trust that he won't try to harm her.
Even though she's never harmed him.
He blew it into such a mess.
When he overreacted and hid.
She doesn't know why.

<u>JUST LIKE THAT</u>

And just like that,
You're gone.
Completely gone
From my life.

And just like that,
I must find a way
To let you go,
Move on,
Forget you.

How did they get there?
To that awful place,
She'd take it all back,
If only she could.

She's stunned that they are there,
Fighting one another,
For what?

How could he think so bad of her?
He misunderstood.
How could he be so nice?
Then so hateful.

Maybe the person she saw all those months
Was a fake,
A ruse.
And this person who hid off camera,
Is really the coward he is,
In the end.

<u>DAZE</u>

I walk around in a daze most of the time.
Wondering how the hell it went so sideways.
How we got to this awful place.
It makes no sense to me at all,
As I sit in a daze.

<u>STOP</u>

She has to stop
Trying to fix it.
Stop apologizing,
Stop wondering,
Stop needing all the answers.

She has to stop
Beating herself up.
Stop blaming it all on herself.
Stop wanting him,
Stop reaching out.

She has to stop,
For her.

BURNT

He burnt that small piece
Of her heart
He stole.
He burnt her soul.
He burnt her kindness
When he twisted her words.
His callousness burnt
Her entire being.

<u>STORM</u>

As she laid down to fall asleep,
Storms rage outside
In the dark.
A different storm rages
In her heart.
And when she awakens,
One will have passed.
While the other
Rages on.

LUST

His eyes on her,
Watching her leave.
She hears his voice,
A sweet sound
Upon her ears.
His hands on her,
Anywhere on her.
His arms holding her,
As they had before.
Their bodies melded as one.
For what seemed like forever.
A perfect moment
In his arms.
Holding him
As he held her.
Their eyes met
She didn't know it was
For the last time.

DR. CHARM

His charm sucked her in.
So deep she was breathless.
His beautiful eyes pierced her soul
With arrows so sharp
She could not break free.
She was hooked.

She was drunk on his charm
With each small sip she tasted.
He never signaled to stop.
He had chances
To push back.
He chose not to.

His wave,
His caresses,
His embrace.
All part of his charm.
It was so powerful,
She drowned in him.

DAYS LIKE TODAY

She hates days like today.
She sits and thinks about what happened.
The ugliness between them.
She never meant any part of this.

On days like today,
She tries to understand
Why he did what he did.
Why he took it to where they are now.
Why he didn't find a way to talk to her.

They shouldn't be here.
Fighting one another.
On days like today,
She wants to call him,
Text him.
But she can't.

REMEMBERING HIM

Sitting at the table,
Sipping her coffee.
She gazed out the window,
Not a cloud in the sky.

As memories float by,
She senses him close.
Her lips curve upward.
Her shoulder tingles.
Her scars itch.

He will always be with her,
No matter how much time passes.
In her memories,
Her scars,
But mostly in her heart,
Where he left the deepest scar of all.

LIES OF THE HEART

She sits at her table reading those papers.
Tears welling up.
She knows one blink and they'll cascade,
Stain her cheeks with pain.
Each lie she reads chips at her heart,
But she reads on and on,
Lie after lie,
Tears falling, splashing onto the papers,
Ruining the ink,
Trying to erase the lies he told.

Her vision blurry,
The lies continue,
Each one a knife into her soul.
When she sees his initials,
More tears break free, burning deeper.
They are the same initials he place on her.

Pain coursing through her,
Her heart shattering within.
She sits still, bowing her head.
Why does he lie?
Why is he so cruel?
All she ever did was care.
Too much,
For him.

WITHOUT ANSWERS

Without answers,
She will dissect this mess,
Forever.
Without answers,
She will relive every moment,
Forever.
Without answers,
This will never end.
It will torment her,
Forever
Without answers.

<u>SCARS</u>

The scars on her shoulder
Are from someone
She held in high regard.
He was kind,
Warm and caring.
Or so she thought.

She sees her scars every damn day,
They're a reminder of him.
For the rest of her days.
In the end,
He was nothing,
Nothing like she thought.

FORBIDDEN

She knew he was forbidden.
For more than one reason.
Many lines were drawn between them.
Some saw them as walls.
They were just lines.
Lines can be crossed,
Walls can be climbed.
She wanted to,
But didn't
She knew he was
Forbidden.

I SHOULDN'T

I was blindsided by it.
Tormented by it.
I denied it even possible.
But that seed planted and grew.
I missed you,
I longed for you.
I wanted you so much.
Yet,
Knowing all along,
I shouldn't.

So, will you meet me?
It's over and done.
Time has gone by.
So, will you see me?
Our lives have moved on.
My only wish is for you to forgive me.
So, will you?

ALONE

She waited for him alone.
Hours passed by.
When she finally saw him,
He broke her,
She was alone.

<u>FINDING WAYS</u>

She's finding ways to heal herself.
She knows it won't be easy.
Slowly, she'll move on,
Time moves forward,
So, she must too.

Letting go is the hardest part.
Finding ways to let go
Will be more difficult.
Only he has the power to help her
Let go quicker, easier.

She hopes he finds a way to reach her.
A way that won't hurt him.
But until that time,
She'll do her best.
Remember the good times,
Try to erase the bad.

When she wants to talk to him,
She'll write it all in a journal.
Maybe one day,
She'll share the entries with him.
One day,
When he finds a way.

GIVE UP

She can't give up
On ever seeing him,
On ever speaking to him,
Again.

She can't give up,
Hoping you find a way,
They find a way,
To talk.

She can't give up
On hope,
On dreams,
On him.

<u>TEARS</u>

I wish you could see me,
See my tear-stained face,
See the immense pain in my eyes.
Feel my heartache.

I can talk to a million people
I only need to talk to you.
Until then,
Tears will fill my life.

<u>ME, MYSELF, & I</u>

Me, myself, and I walked into your office.
Waiting patiently for you.
The door swung open and in you came.
Me, myself, and I smiled as you introduced yourself.
I noticed how beautiful you were.
My eyes were fixated on you as you sat before me.
Me, myself, and I saw the gold wedding band.
I reigned myself in immediately.
Dammit, you're married,
So
Me,
Myself,
& I
Calmed the fuck down.

She opens her phone,
Finds the special app,
The one that holds their photos.

She goes there to see him.
When she really misses him.

His smile,
His eyes,
His arm around her,
Her hand resting on his hip.
That day lives on in their photos.

<u>CALL</u>

Remember your text to me?
"Can I call you tomorrow?"
It feels like eons ago.

I should've taken your call.
I wish I would've taken your call.
I need you to call me now,
Please call.

Cry
It's all she seems to do.
She'll cry whenever
She thinks about it,
She'll cry whenever
She thinks about why.
She'll cry whenever
She thinks about how.
She'll cry whenever
She thinks about him.
She'll cry whenever
She talks about it.
She'll just cry.

<u>WAITING</u>

She's there waiting.
It's grueling,
The waiting.
She has to wait,
She can't do this anymore.
She needs answers.
He has them.
She'll wait and wait and wait.
To speak with him.
She has to wait.

How was she so wrong about him?
He seemed so strong,
But is so weak.

She just wants to talk.
He tells her he can't.
She asked him why?
He tells her he's happy she's doing well.
She begs him to please tell her why he can't.
He repeats,
"I can't talk to you"
Over and over.

She leaves that night
Broken once again.
How was she so wrong about him?

SOULS

Her soul felt his.
She knew they connected on a different level.
When they first met, he reached into the deepest part of
her soul.
He touched parts of her no one has ever reached before.

Her soul was on fire for his.
She knew his soul met hers.
They shared their truest side.
Their souls found the other,
But life tore them apart.

One day she will try to begin moving on.
She doesn't know when.
Maybe tomorrow,
The next day, next week,
Next month, next year.
Or maybe never.

She doesn't know when she'll begin moving on.
But she knows she is forever changed by him.
Meeting him,
Getting to know him,
And profoundly changed by his actions.
His heartlessness,
His cowardliness
But mostly,
His lies.

SHE'S LOST

The man she needs to talk with,
Says he can't.
She's lost without knowing why.
The man she needs to explain things to
Ignores her pleas.
She's lost in all the pain this has caused.
"Please,"
She cries out.
"Please see me."
She can't move on without talking to him,
She's lost in this chaos.

I wish I could turn back time.
Go back to the last time we were together.
Never share my work with you.
Go back to a time before our misunderstanding.
That's all it was,
I swear.

In this time, we are in,
My heart aches from
The pain this has caused.
I want to go back in time.
Back to a time when I thought you cared.

<u>I MISS YOU</u>

I miss seeing you.
I miss our time together.
We talked about why I was there first,
Then our usual friendly chats.

Your body spoke to mine.
We exchanged a wave,
We shared an embrace.
We shared something special,
We did.

It was something so damn special,
It scared you.
But it didn't scare me.
I miss you.

<u>CANYON</u>

There's a canyon between us.
Where once there was just a line.
The line was never crossed by either.
I won't lie,
I wanted to cross that line.

Now that line has been removed,
It's been replaced by a canyon.
A divide so great,
I'm not sure it can be filled.

I will try my best to remove the wall,
The divide,
The canyon,
That others have placed in our way.

If it's meant to be, it will be,
Or I will set you free.
I will let go,
I will move on.

But not without trying absolutely everything
I have within my power,
To see you again.

REGRETS

Her biggest regret,
Not telling him everything
When they were alone.

She had so much to say,
She wants to tell him,
Every last thing.

She wants no regrets
In her life,
But this one is huge.

Would things be different
Had she told him that day?
Maybe, she would've known his answers.
He would've known hers.

Until they speak,
She'll have regrets.

THE WORST TIME

The worst time is when she's alone.
He enters her thoughts,
She tries hard to distract herself,
But he's there.

She remembers when he said,
Come by anytime,
Say hi, visit
But wait until the pandemic has passed.

She wishes it were true.
She would stop by in a heartbeat.
But she know she can't
Even when the pandemic is gone.

That will be the worst time for her.
Knowing she messed it all up.
Wanting to see him,
Spend time with him.

The worst time is now,
Knowing he is so close,
Wishing they could talk,
Trying to forget him.
That's something
She'll never be able to do.

<u>LIGHT</u>

Light returned when I realized who you are.
I'm not shackled by your lies anymore.
Light has taught me to stand in my truth.
Light has shown me,
Who I am,
What I'm worth,
How I will succeed,
Despite you.
The truth will come out.
Into the light,
For all to know.

<u>STRUGGLED</u>

She struggled today,
Endured through a meltdown.
She cried over him
For the first time in a while.
She still needs him
To hear her,
To see her.

She knows she was just a number to him.
She knows that now.
She never mattered
To him.
He made her believe
She had.

But in reality,
He fooled her.
His kindness
Was fake,
His caring touch,
Just a tease.

She struggled today
Because
He
Broke
Her.

<u>KEY</u>

Without a key to my heart,
You shattered it,
Crushed it,
Completely demolished me.

Without a key to my heart,
You managed to rip it from my chest.
Throw it on the ground,
And stomp the beats from it.

<u>PLEASE TALK TO ME</u>

That's all I'm asking,
I don't give a shit
What I violate.
I'm asking you to
Please talk to me.

<u>WHEN</u>

When will it stop?
Her heart is,
Shattered,
Broken,
Devastated,
Hurt.
In a sea of pain.
An ocean of regret.
Please forgive her.
When will she heal?

I LOST MY MIND

I lost my mind over you.
Your charm made me drunk on you,
Your smile melted me,
Your eyes, fuck, just fuck.
Your voice was music to me,
The way you seemed to care for me,
I lost my way into you.
Your touch sent shockwaves through me.
Connecting sensations, I felt every day.
Your arms around me
Mine around you.
That's the day,
I lost my mind over you.

<u>FEELINGS</u>

Love, lust, desire.
Wanting, infatuation.
All the above.
It began with one,
Grew into the next,
With each passing month,
It became stronger.
Did he play her?
She didn't feel that.
Was he playing with her?
It seemed that way to her.
It he still?

She's drowning in pain,
Sorrow, heartbreak, silence.
She cried in pain, from loss.
She's tempted to drown herself in whiskey.
It will numb her pain
Temporarily mend what's broken.
She knows better.
Instead, she does her best to heal.
Not knowing when she will,
If ever.

<u>TRAGEDY</u>

A tragedy inside me
My mind moves on,
My heart refuses.

A moment is all she asked him for.
To talk, to fix their misunderstanding.
Nothing more.

A moment like he gave her before.
She needs to settle things between them.
His silence has done great harm to her.

Her erratic behavior stems from his refusal.
She tried over and over for a moment.
Not for the reasons he assumes.

A moment for forgiveness,
A moment to begin healing herself.
A moment to begin the rest of her life.

LOST

Lost in a sea of WTF?
A year ago
Excitement filled me.
Ready to move forward
A daring adventure.
Ready to play.
Now I'm just lost,
Searching for closure,
Finding none.

I CAN'T BELIEVE

I can't believe
I'll never see you again.
I'll never speak with you again.

I can't believe
Where we ended up.
How things went so bad.

I can't believe
You're just a memory now,
You're gone from my life.

<u>PIECE OF ME</u>

My heart shattered,
When you refused to see me.
When everyone ignored
My calls for help.

Time moves on,
I still hope we can talk one day.
But for now,
I leave a little piece of me
A small dot of hope,
In that corner of my heart,
Where you still are.

PAIN

The pain is unbearable,
It rips through her body.
He wasn't what she thought.
He wasn't even close.
Beware of those with charm,
They will draw you in,
Then toss you out.
Their ego is more important,
Then your heart ever was.

FOOL (ed)

Was she a fool for thinking he was interested?
Or was she fooled by him?
Could it be a bit of both?
Maybe.
But either way,
Fool is part of what happened.
Whether she was a fool, or he fooled her,
It falls at her feet.
She owns it all.
Every mistake,
She owns them.
She lives in truth.
She wishes she knew,
Which she was,
Only he knows that answer.
But he has a problem with the truth.

HEART AND DREAMS

As long as you have a spot in my heart,
As long as you come to me in my dreams,
As long as this mess stays unresolved,
I won't be able to let go,
Or move on.

I can busy myself,
Distract myself.
Do all kinds of things to keep you away.
But as long as you are in my heart,
You show up in my dreams.

NIGHTMARE

It turned into a nightmare.
All she asked for was one meeting.
Just one.
Silence,
Deafening silence.
She reached out,
She was ignored.
She kept trying to reach him.
She made the ultimate mistake.
She believed she mattered to him.
Now she knows
She doesn't matter.
She'll pick up the pieces,
She'll figure out her life.
She'll never trust like that again.

My soul is dead.
My mind burns.
My eyes ache.
The tears scorch my cheeks.
My head throbs,
My heart is bruised.
My body hurts.

<u>I MISS …</u>

I miss…
Talking to you,
Even though you didn't respond.
I still talked to you.

I miss…
Seeing you,
Even though I knew it would end,
When my year was over.

I miss…
That chance for a friendship,
A unique one between us.
That's what I wanted.

I miss…
That beautiful,
Special man
Who's inside you.

I miss…
Our connection,
Yes, we had one,
You know we did.

I miss…
It all.

<u>TROUBLE</u>

Trying everything,
Reaching out,
Over and over.
Unable to see the danger,
Believing it will work out.
Leaving common sense behind as
Each attempt made things worse.

In the end,
It spelled
TROUBLE

<u>ATTRACTION</u>

Her attraction to him came from nowhere.
She awoke and there he was.
Her fantasy was front and center,
He was real.
She could touch him,
But did she dare?

With each passing month,
Her attraction grew deeper,
She sensed him more often.
Every day and every night.
They touched in her dreams.
He touched her heart.
She was completely under his spell.

MIDDLE

The place where he began was
The exact middle of her dreams.
He stayed there night after night.
Then he moved to the exact middle
Of her thoughts
Twenty-four-seven.
He drove her wild.

Soon he moved into
The exact middle of her heart,
In time he tore it apart with his lies.
Then she had to move herself back into
The exact middle of her soul
And move him out.

<u>WATCH</u>

She saw him watch her,
When she left his office.
Did he watch her
Every time?

He watched her change
Before his very eyes.
In all aspects of her life.
He seemed interested.
Was that just his charm?

She watched as his arms reached for her.
And she embraced him.
That memory is so vivid.
So beautiful for her.
He holding her
She holding him.
In his arms,
She felt safe.

Then he dropped
A bomb
Into her life.
And watched her implode.

<u>HANDS OF TIME</u>

Turn back the hands of time,
To before the day,
She made her mistake.
To when they had a chance at something.
To when they spoke.
Turn back the hands of time,
Because she needs him in her life,
He already lives in her heart.

<u>FATE</u>

Was it fate that brought him into her life?
Or a cruel trick?
For sixteen months,
It seemed surreal.
She looked forward to those days.
To see him, talk with him.
Then she made a mistake.
Was that fate too?
Fate brought him to her,
Then took him from her.

<u>DIAMOND IN THE SAND</u>

I remember the day we met.
I thought I found a diamond in the sand.
Your smile was so bright.
Your eyes danced when they met mine.
With each passing month,
What I thought to be true,
Became what I knew,
I found a diamond in the sand,
In you.

<u>BARELY BREATHE</u>

She can barely breathe.
The pain from him is crushing her soul.
She can barely breathe.
His meanness towards her is debilitating.
She can barely breathe.
His stubbornness is beyond ridiculous.
She can barely breathe.
His callousness is beyond the pale.
She can barely breathe.
He has nearly killed her with his ugliness.
She can barely breathe.

PARADOX

His body language was a paradox to his actions he took
against her.
His touch was soft,
His embrace, tender.
His lies burned her soul,
He hides so she cannot see his eyes.
A deep love grew,
Her own self lives in a paradox of emotions for him.

AFRAID

People lie because they are afraid.
Who were you afraid of?
Why did you lie so much?
Afraid of me? Please
It wasn't me you're afraid of.
It's someone,
But not me.

How did we get here?
A question,
I ask you.
Because only you know,
Only you can give me that answer.

Is this really who you are?
Callous,
Hateful,
Unforgiving?

So, please,
Tell me,
How did we get here?

<u>THE V</u>

She loved to connect with him through his beautiful blue
eyes.
She held onto his gaze for as long as he held hers.
Each time they met,
The connection became deeper,
Stronger.

The V though,
Oh my,
The V in his scrubs.
That opening where she could see a spattering of his
brown chest hair.
Just the right amount.
As her fingers brushed across the V, In her mind.

She'd dream of her hands
Tumbling down his firm body,
Bumping over his abs.
Feeling the soft brown hair
Feathering through her fingertips.
Through his trail,
To her treasure.

ONE HEART

How can one heart be full of love,
Yet broken at the same time?
Her heart beats full of love,
Yet lays shredded inside her chest.
Love and sorrow thread through her heart.
One heart,
Loving so deeply,
And crying so loudly to be heard.

Yes, I'm sad, but I'll be fine.
Yes, he meant something to me.
In time that will fade away.

Yes, I was fooled, but never again.
Yes, I thought he cared about me,
But now I know it was just an act.
Yes, I should've known better,
Yes, I've learned a hard lesson.

But I hope,
For his sake,
He learned one too.

<u>WOULD YOU</u>

Would you,
If you saw her,
Say, "Hello"
Or would you walk
The other way?
She'd say "Hello"
Because she believes in being kind,
Even to you.

<u>WORDS</u>

Words
matter.
Choose
yours
 carefully.

<u>FORGET</u>

She wants to forget him,
So, she feels no pain.
Forget his lies,
Forget the way he watched her,
Forget the way he smiled at her,
Forget the way he looked at her,
Forget the way he embraced her.
That last time alone,
Before it exploded.
Forget him.

WORN OUT

He's worn her out.
Mentally,
She's worn out.
Physically spent.
He's crushed her.
Emotionally shattered,
Worn out.

<u>NOT THERE</u>

No, not there.
I can't see you there.
I want to see you,
So very much,
But not there.

<u>SERENDIPITY</u>

She wasn't looking for anything.
Her life was good,
She was happy.

Then they met.
And everything changed.
She needed him,
He helped her.

A spark ignited between them.
She saw it in his eyes,
Felt it in his touch,
Say what you will,
You were her
Serendipity.

Hope.
It's all she has left.
Hope,
He will one day find her.
Hope,
He will one day talk to her.
Hope,
One day he will see her.
Hope,
One day they forgive each other.
Hope,
One day they confess their truths.
Hope,
It's all she has left.

<u>YOU</u>

<u>PART ONE</u>

Could things get better as time goes on?
And one day we meet and make amends.
Say it is a possibility, please.
Everyone makes mistakes and
You will need someone's forgiveness too.

PART TWO

Remember me but.
Only because you want to.
Good times can still be had,
Every chance we may take,
Right time, right place, in the future.

<u>HURT</u>

The hurt is deep.
Cuts like a knife,
Slicing her heart into ribbons.
He tells lies,
He hurt her
Like no other.

<u>WILL YOU EVER</u>

Will you ever
Be man enough?
Will you ever
Have the courage?
Will you ever
Be honest?
Will you ever
Be kind to me?
Will you ever
Stop hiding?

<u>SCREAM</u>

Fuck!
I want to scream!
I need to scream!
Throw something.
Break something.
I'm so frustrated,
So infuriated,
Fucking mad!

IDK ANYMORE

What happened?
Why can't you?
Will you someday?
IDK anymore.
I'm still lost,
Still hoping,
Still wanting.

<u>A LOVE LOST</u>

Unconventional to say the least.
A love lost that hit like a bus.
Unexpected,
But a love that was real.
Tormented by not knowing
But feeling there was something.
Something nice,
Risky,
And fun.

It would be much easier
To talk to me.
Instead of trolling me.
Seriously,
It would settle everything.
I promise.

<u>SPACES</u>

Sad space,
Mad space,
Tired space,
Love space,
Hate space.

Spin the bottle to what space she sits in today.
Some days the space stays the same,
Other days, she runs the gamut.
Very few days she is in the nothing space.

She wants to be in the done space.
Perfect scenario, the mess is resolved, forgiven, said
goodbye space.

But that space takes bravery to enter.
She's ready to go there,
Hash it all out,
But he's not.

She'll continue to play spin the space bottle,
Until something gives.
What will it be?
He holds all the cards.
Hold on or let go.
Time to choose.

THE PLEASURE OF YOU

You-Me
A sinful secret.
When you held me,
I knew you wanted it too.

The excitement,
The desire,
Shhh,
The pleasure of you.

Alas, it's just a dream.
A want that lives on,
A wishful fantasy unfulfilled.
Of you and me.

<u>ONE YEAR AGO</u>

One year ago today,
She trusted him with her dream.
She felt safe enough to share with him.
His vibe came to her strong that day.
A deep connection of caring,
Trust,
A mutual interest.

When she left him that afternoon,
She still felt all that between them.

One year ago, today
She went out on a limb,
Skated on thin ice,
Went for the platinum ring.
That was him.

<u>END</u>

He was
Someone special
Who turned out
To be
absolutely awful.
Looking so perfect
Keeping her hopeful
Every month
Right to the end.

FRIENDSHIP

It's what she wanted.
A friendship.
She knew it would be special.
Her feelings ran deeper,
But knew a friendship was all they could share.

She controlled her heart,
She wanted him in her life.
He was special,
He still is.

She needs him to understand,
A friendship was it.
She'll bide her time,
Wait for things to calm down,
She doesn't know when,
But one day,
She'll reach out to him,
To be friends.

<u>FINISHED</u>

It's over, done,
Finished.
He broke her for the last time.
She wanted to clear up the mess.
No one cared how this affected her.
Misunderstanding
turned to chaos.

She tried and failed,
Every damn time.
She was ignored,
She was accused.
All she wanted,
Was to fix the mess.
She wanted it finished,
And now it is.

<u>GOODBYE</u>

I never expected to say goodbye so soon.
You were such an important part of my life.
I was sure we could remain friends when our professional
relationship ended.
That's what I wanted.

A stop by and say 'hi'
Or meet for lunch every so often.
A text to check in.

The chasm between us now is so great that a friendship is
unlikely.
The misunderstanding grew into such a mess.
We probably cannot come back from.

The scars from my surgery are permanent and a daily
reminder of you.
The scars on my heart and mind may fade over time.
You'll become a memory,
Good and bad.
I'll do my best to remember the good and forget the bad.

Please know when you read this poem,
It is for you.
Just this one though,
Don't let your ego get the best of you.

I cared for you,
I trusted you,
I thought you were kind,
Worth my efforts to try and fix what went horribly wrong.

In the end,
I saw your real self.
You damaged me,
By lying and restricting me.

One damn meeting,
It would've ended it all then.
I promise it would have.
So now it's goodbye.
KC

Thank you to my husband for his continued love and
support in all my new endeavors.
I love you, baby.

This poetry book is dedicated to all of us who are struggling to be seen and heard.
For those who seek forgiveness and never know if it was granted.
For those that forgive, but never forget.
Always be your biggest cheerleader.
Never give up on yourself, keep reaching for the stars, baby.

EB Taylor lives in Florida with her husband. They spend time with family and friends and look forward to their vacations in Las Vegas.
EB uses her poetry for therapy. To release the pain, capture the joy, and write it all out for all to enjoy.